ARCHIMEDES

The Father of Mathematics

THE LIBRARY OF GREEK PHILOSOPHERS™

ARCHIMEDES

The Father of Mathematics

Heather Hasan

The Rosen Publishing Group, Inc., New York

To Ray and Lena Francis (Nana and Pop-Pop). Many of my fondest childhood memories involve the two of you. Please know that you are greatly loved and cherished.

Published in 2006 by The Rosen Publishing Group, Inc.
29 East 21st Street, New York, NY 10010

First Edition

Library of Congress Cataloging-in-Publication Data

Hasan, Heather.
Archimedes: the father of mathematics / Heather Hasan.
    p. cm.—(The library of Greek philosophers)
ISBN 1-4042-0774-0 (lib. bdg.)
1. Archimedes—Juvenile literature. 2. Mathematicians—Greece—Biography—Juvenile literature.
I. Title. II. Series.
QA29.A7H37 2005
510'.92—dc22

                                                          2005009992

Printed in China

On the cover: A nineteenth-century bust of Archimedes. Background: *Cicero Discovering the Tomb of Archimedes* by Benjamin West.

CONTENTS

INTRODUCTION

Archimedes was born in Syracuse. Syracuse is situated on the coast of the island of Sicily, which is in the Mediterranean Sea. Though Syracuse is now part of Italy, it was part of Greece at the time of Archimedes' birth. The first people recorded to have inhabited Sicily were the Sicans. These people were living on the island by 10,000 BC, or about 12,000 years ago. The Sicans were driven to the western and southern parts of the island by the Sicels, who gave Sicily its name. Because of Sicily's good geographical position for trade and the wonderful fertility of its soil, the island attracted many navigators. Among them were the Phoenicians, who originated from the coast of North Africa, and the Greeks.

Around 733 BC, Greek colonists from Corinth (in southern Greece) built the city of Syracuse on the eastern coast of Sicily, driving the native Sicels from that area. From there, Syracuse grew rapidly. The Corinthian Greeks moved westward, and, in 691 BC, they also settled Gela, an area on the southwestern coast of the island. By 635 BC, the Greeks had successfully driven the Phoenicians to the western part of the island, an area near what is known today as Palermo. Eventually, Sicily became home to more Greeks than Greece itself.

Sicily prospered under the rule of the Greeks. This prosperity was the result of trade, both by land and sea. Syracuse entered the fifth century BC as the strongest and most important of all the Greek cities of Sicily. However, Syracuse's vast wealth and resources invited conquest, and, for years, the people of Syracuse had to fight off raids.

During this time, Syracuse also faced repeated conflicts with the Phoenicians. After arriving in western Sicily, the Phoenicians had intermarried with the native people of that area. Over the years, they became known as the Carthaginians, or the Punics. The word "punic" comes from the Greek word *phoinikos*, which means "purple," and which

During Archimedes' time, Syracuse, on the eastern coast of what is now Sicily, was a city in great transition. King Hiero II was in constant conflict with invaders, namely the Romans, which eventually led to the Punic Wars. The Punic Wars left Sicily in the hands of Rome. Syracuse, however, remained an independent Greek city. Archimedes, along with many other great historians, mathematicians, geographers, and linguists, was influenced by this turbulent time, which came to be known as the Hellenistic period. This detail from a sixteenth-century fresco (*inset*) shows the city of Syracuse.

GREEK AND CA
COLONIZATIO
AND SOUTHE

Panormus : Carthaginian c
Syracuse: Greek colony
Boundary of Ca

0   20   40

Ⓐ

Drepanum   Panc

•Segesta

•Lilybaeum   Hypsus

Mazara   •Selinus

Heraclea Minoa•

Acragas•
(Agrigent

M E

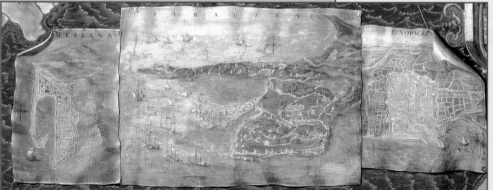

territory

30 miles

TYRRHENIAN

SEA

Laus
Cerilli
Thurii
Sybaris
(destroyed 510 B.C.)

Consentia

Croton

GRAECIA

Hipponium
Scyllecium

Liparaeae Is.

Lipara

Metaurum
Caulonia

Scyllaeum
Messana

Mylae

Locri

Tyndaris

Mytistratum

STRAIT OF MESSINA

Rhegium

MAGNA

Etna

Tauromenium
Naxus

IONIAN SEA

Symaithus

Gelas

Catana

Eryces
Leontini
Megara

Anapus

ela

Syracuse
Acrae

marina

RRANEAN

SEA

probably referred to the purple dye that was produced in the area. The Syracusans and the Carthaginians fought constantly to expel each other from Sicily.

For centuries, Syracuse swung back and forth between a democracy and a dictatorship. The idea of democracy, or government ruled by the people, was first introduced to the world by the Greeks. Their ideas of democracy, trial by jury, and equality under the law formed the foundation on which Western civilization was built. However, in between the times of democracy were times of dictatorship, in which the people

As a testament to the great changes that were taking place in Archimedes' Syracuse, the Phoenicians heavily influenced the population of Sicily. Having intermarried with the native people, they created a whole new race, the Carthaginians, also known as the Punics. Shown here is a Phoenician merchant ship carved onto the side of a sarcophagus, or tomb, from the Phoenician city of Sidon.

were ruled by the decisions of one man. The men who ruled Syracuse during these times of dictatorship were known as tyrants. The word "tyrant" does not carry as negative a meaning in Greek as it does in English. These rulers were called tyrants because they ascended to power through the use of force.

In the late third century BC, a group of Italian mercenaries, who had been hired by the Greeks, seized the town of Messana (modern-day Messina). Messana was strategically located on the straits separating Sicily from Italy. These mercenaries, or hired soldiers, called themselves Mamertines. This name may have been derived from the Oscan name for Mars, the god of war. The Oscans were people of ancient Italy occupying Campania. They used the town of Messana as a base for raiding nearby towns, and Syracuse was located dangerously close. In 269 BC, a new tyrant, King Hiero II, emerged in Syracuse. He ruled from about 270 BC to 215 BC (much of Archimedes' adult life). Hiero attacked the Mamertines in order to protect Syracuse. The Mamertines, in turn, appealed to Rome for assistance.

At that time, the Romans controlled much of what is now Italy. The Carthaginians, not wanting the Romans to intervene in Sicily, sent naval and ground forces to Messana. The Mamertines accepted help from

Carthage, forcing King Hiero to withdraw. After some time, however, the requested Roman forces also arrived in Messana. When the armies from Rome and Carthage met, war erupted. This marked the beginning of the first of three wars known collectively as the Punic Wars, which were fought between the Romans and the Carthaginians. These long and exhausting conflicts greatly affected both Archimedes' life and his work.

During the First Punic War (264–241 BC), Syracuse initially supported Carthage. However, early in the war, Rome forced a treaty of alliance from King Hiero. At the end of the war, the Carthaginians and the Romans signed a treaty in which Carthage gave up Sicily. Rome made the rest of Sicily a province but left Syracuse as an independent Greek city. It was in this atmosphere that Archimedes lived out most of his life.

The time period into which Archimedes was born has come to be known as the Hellenistic period (323–30 BC). The word "Hellenistic" is derived from *Hellenes*, which is simply the Greek word for "Greek." The Hellenistic period began with the death of Alexander the Great in 323 BC, and ended with Rome's occupation of the last major Hellenistic kingdom in approximately 30 BC. The Hellenistic period was marked by the spread of Greek ideas and culture. A Greek dialect became common, and was the language used for trade and commerce. The Greeks tended to view anyone who spoke their language and shared in their customs as part of their culture. The Greeks had a great influence on the people of their time, and this influence continues even into modern times. The Greeks shaped our laws, our arts, and our sciences. They also laid the foundation for our ethical standards, or how we view right and wrong.

During the Hellenistic period, pretty much every aspect of life flourished, including the arts and the economy. Hellenistic art, mostly sculptures, have survived to this day. Painting was also important, but not much remains besides copies made by the Romans. The Hellenistic period was a time of naturalistic art. The art was very expressive, often showing violently constricted bodies displaying great emotion. Much of the literature that existed during the Hellenistic period was poetry. The Greeks developed tragedy, comedy, and lyric (songlike) poetry. Theocritus of Syracuse was known for his writing of pastoral idyll and bucolic poems—short, descriptive poems about country life. Many of his poems survive today.

A number of philosophies existed during the Hellenistic period. Many Hellenistic people practiced a philosophy called humanism. Also known as man-worship, humanism focuses on the needs and interests of people. Many philosophers of the time focused on achieving peace of mind. The Epicurean philosophers believed that it is best to have a little pleasure and very little pain. Another philosophy called Stoicism held the idea that a divine mind controlled the world and planned the course of people's lives. Stoics believed that happiness resulted when people grasped this idea and simply tried to live their already planned lives as best they could. The Cynics, who practiced a philosophy called Cynicism, tried to disregard all pleasures and desires, seeking only to live virtuously.

The Hellenistic period is also known for its advances in science, and great advances were made in astronomy and mathematics. During this period, the Greeks began observing the universe around them, questioning the mathematical certainty of life, and proposing new ideas. In fact, the Greeks questioned just about everything. Before the Greeks, there was really no true science. The Egyptians practiced science, but it was only a practical science. For them, everything needed to serve a purpose. The Greeks, however, loved knowledge for its own sake. Many of the discoveries that the Greeks made were of no

Among Archimedes' Greek peers, who were likewise influenced by the great transitions and radical thinking of the Hellenistic period, was Euclid, represented in this 1334 carving. Euclid was known for his work in establishing the mathematics of geometry. Both Euclid and Archimedes, who are among the greatest thinkers the world has ever known, emerged from relatively the same time and place in history.

practical use to them. Much of it was lost, not to be uncovered for hundreds of years. Once rediscovered, however, much of what they had learned became the beginnings of modern science and philosophy.

Many great thinkers lived during the Hellenistic period. These include the historian Polybius; the mathematician Euclid, who is almost singlehandedly responsible for modern geometry; the geographers Eratosthenes (he accurately calculated the circumference of Earth) and Poseidonius; and the linguist Dionysius Thrax. However, no list of great Hellenistic thinkers

would be complete if it did not include Archimedes. In one of the greatest civilizations ever and among some of the most brilliant thinkers, he still stands out from all the rest. He was undoubtedly one of the most intelligent people in history. In the following chapters, we will travel through the life, the education, and the discoveries of this great mathematician Archimedes.

1 THE LIFE OF ARCHIMEDES

Archimedes, considered by many to be the father of mathematics, was born around 287 BC. Many historians rank Archimedes with Sir Isaac Newton and Carl Friedrich Gauss as one of the three greatest mathematicians who ever lived. However, very little is known about the early life of this great man. In fact, it is quite surprising how very little is known about the life of Archimedes at all. Archimedes himself never wrote about his life, and only one biography is known to have been written about him in his time. It was authored by Archimedes' friend Heracleides. Sadly, this work is lost. Though not much is known about the personal life of Archimedes, it is indisputable that he changed the course of scientific history.

This 1630 portrait of Archimedes was created by the artist Jusepe de Ribera. In this painting, Archimedes is holding a compass, and is apparently working on a mathematical problem. Also evidenced in the painting is a halo-like hue encircling Archimedes' head, an artistic device de Ribera used to express his subject's divine-like intellect.

ARCHIMEDES' EARLY EDUCATION

Unlike those of Newton and Gauss, Archimedes' background and upbringing probably steered him directly into the field of mathematics. It is safe to assume that Archimedes was aware of the importance of precise mathematics from an early age. For one, Archimedes' father, Pheidias, had been a well-known astronomer and mathematician. This surely gave Archimedes an interest in science. This may also explain why Archimedes found the sun, the moon, and the planets so fascinating.

Archimedes was born into the leisured, upper class. Historians believe that, as a child from an educated, upper-class family, Archimedes would have received a thorough grounding in mathematics as part of his education. The Greeks loved knowledge, and they sent their sons to school to become knowledgeable Greek citizens. In school, it is likely that Archimedes was exposed to knowledge originating in Egypt, Babylon, and Greece.

Historians believe that Archimedes would have learned the letters of the Greek alphabet. These letters also doubled as numerals (a little mark next to the letter showed the reader that the letter was being

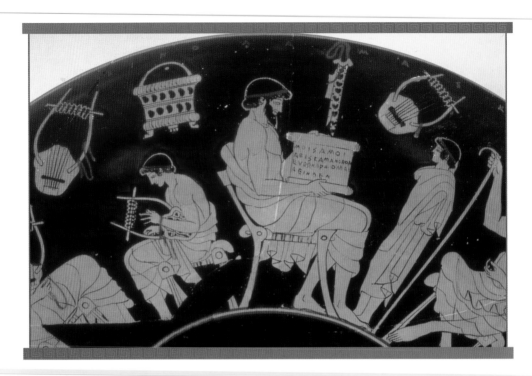

Knowledge and physical well-being were critical elements in the upbringing of the ancient Greeks. Greek youths were given an all-encompassing education, involving the study of a wide range of subjects and intensive physical education, as this illustration of a teacher with his student shows.

used as a number). He would have studied Homer, a poet who wrote history; Solon, who wrote about the law; and Aesop, who wrote fables. In addition to astronomy, he also would have studied music and drawing. He would have been taught military strategy and how to use weapons, too. Since the Greeks believed that a good mind needed a strong body, Archimedes would have also learned how to wrestle, box, run, jump, and throw a spear. Also, he would have learned how to swim and dive.

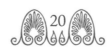

Writing in the Dirt

When speaking about Archimedes, some scholars will mention his tendency to write on whatever surfaces he could find. Anything and everything served as a writing surface for Archimedes. He scrawled ideas on sawdust-covered floors and drew geometric shapes in the ashes of extinguished fires. However, Archimedes did have other options.

(continued on following page)

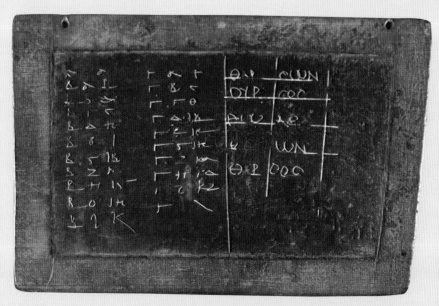

Most of Archimedes' drawings and ideas are forever lost literally to the sands of time because Archimedes made all his calculations in the sand and dirt itself. Papyrus and wax tablets, such as this, were too expensive. However, if Archimedes' writings had somehow been preserved, they would be invaluable to us today as insight into his mind and work.

(continued from previous page)

As a child in school, he would have been given a wax-covered wooden tablet on which to write. On it he would have scratched his letters with a sharp, pointed iron graver. When he was able to write very well, Archimedes would have been given papyrus to write on. His pen would have been made from a reed, and the ink he dipped it in would have been made of gum and soot. Books were also surprisingly popular and common among the Greeks, even though the printing press would not be invented for another 1,700 years.

Why, then, did Archimedes spend hours sitting on the ground, drawing his diagrams in the dirt? The answer is, most geometers in his day worked like that. They had no pencils or erasers. Each sheet of papyrus was made by hand and was too valuable just to be scribbled on and then thrown away. Also, it was difficult to change a diagram that had been cut into clay or scratched into a wax surface. It turns out that a surface of dirt, sand, or ash was ideal for drawing in this time when paper was scarce. With a simple sweep of his hand, Archimedes was able to smooth away any mistakes and start fresh with a new diagram.

During the third century BC, Syracuse was the hub for commerce, science, and art. In the days of Archimedes, as many as 500,000 people lived in Syracuse. In fact, it was one of the largest cities in the

ancient world. Archimedes probably walked through the crowded markets, packed with merchants selling books and other goods, up the narrow, busy streets, and down to the prosperous shipyards filled with workers. He may have stood on the docks packed with Greek ships and watched as they were coming and going from places like Egypt and Athens. Growing up in such a rich area would have definitely helped Archimedes to develop natural curiosity and fondness for solving problems.

Archimedes would surely become some sort of mathematician in this social and economic order of things. Whether he would become a brilliant one or a bumbling amateur was to be seen. However, time would reveal that Archimedes was to become not only gifted in the field of mathematics, but also a genius.

THE ROYAL FAMILY OF SYRACUSE

Many historians agree that Archimedes belonged to the nobility of Syracuse and that his family was in some way related to Hiero II, the king of Syracuse. Whether the families were related, Archimedes certainly had an intimate relationship with Hiero and his son, Gelon, both of whom had the utmost respect for him.

During Archimedes' day, politics was tied to the arts and sciences. King Hiero II of Syracuse, as rendered on this bronze coin, had a strong bond with Archimedes and was partly responsible for the mathematician's success. Hiero II led a peaceful reign, during which he rebuilt much of Syracuse and won the hearts of its citizens. One of these citizens was Archimedes. Hiero II's peaceful reign allowed the mathematician to focus on his intellectual pursuits.

King Hiero II ruled Syracuse from about 270 BC to 215 BC, almost the entire span of Archimedes' adult life. Hiero was a peace-loving ruler in a time when rulers were often prone to war. In fact, many historians believe that Hiero was able to finish out his rule without ever killing, injuring, or exiling a single citizen. Hiero built temples, a theater, and new fortifications all, according to reports, without having to tax his citizens heavily. The beginning of Hiero's rule marked a golden age for Syracuse. The treaty that Hiero had negotiated with Rome during the First Punic War ensured a peaceful and prosperous reign for Hiero as well as for the people of Syracuse.

Greek Mythology

Greek mythology is based on traditional tales of gods and heroes. Some Greeks recognized that the stories were fictional. However, the majority of the Greek people viewed them as true. The people of Syracuse looked to Artemis, the Greek goddess of the hunt, as their main deity. They believed that Artemis had the power to heal as well as send mortals into sudden death. According to tradition, she was the protector of the young and presided over childbirth. Artemis, also called the Maiden of the Silver Bow, hunted with silver arrows; hounds accompanied her while she hunted. Artemis was so important to the people of Syracuse that they had a bronze coin made that bore the image of her with an arrow over her shoulder.

Artemis, the Greek goddess of wild animals and the hunt, is depicted here with a deer in this marble statue from the first or second century AD. In Greek mythology, Artemis is the daughter of Letu and Zeus, and twin sister of Apollo. The statue here depicts her as a hunter, as evidenced by the arrows she holds on her back, and the stag at her side.

This oil painting by Sebastiano Ricci is an example of Hiero II's close relationship with Archimedes. The painting depicts Hiero II sitting on the horse and calling upon Archimedes, to whom Hiero II is pointing, to help him fortify the city of Syracuse. Hiero II frequently sought Archimedes' advice on such intellectual matters as military strategy.

Hiero's long reign had a major impact on the life of Archimedes, for Hiero gave him the opportunity to pursue his studies. Whenever Hiero faced a difficult situation, he sought Archimedes' help. The king asked Archimedes questions about everything from military matters to sailing issues. It seems that Archimedes made a hobby out of solving the king's most difficult problems. Some of the questions posed by the king may have even led Archimedes to some of his greatest discoveries.

Archimedes undoubtedly gained a lot of knowledge as a boy in Syracuse. However, when he had learned as much as he could there, Archimedes left Sicily to study in Alexandria, Egypt's northernmost port city located at the mouth of the Nile River. Archimedes was still quite young when he made the journey to Alexandria. This was the only time in his life that he ventured from his beloved home in Syracuse.

Archimedes had to sail across the Mediterranean Sea in order to reach Alexandria. Although the Greeks were known to be good sailors, sea travel was still a very dangerous thing. Greek ships were small, wooden vessels called round ships. These round ships had a stationary square sail, which could not be turned into the direction of the wind.

Therefore, the crew was forced to sail in whatever direction the wind was blowing. Also, the ships did not have keels, the central framing part on the bottom of a ship that keeps it steady in the sea. Sailors

This mosaic of the city of Alexandria from St. John's Church in Gerasa, Jordan, is from the sixth century AD, 300 years after the city was founded by Alexander the Great. That such artwork was being created so long after the founding of the city is a sign of just how important the metropolis was. Alexandria grew to be a great cultural center of learning.

had no compasses or charts to guide them, and the Mediterranean Sea was full of pirates. It probably took sixteen or seventeen days for Archimedes to reach his destination. Going to Alexandria must have meant a lot to him—he risked so much to get there. However, knowing Archimedes' great thirst for knowledge, it is not surprising that he was willing to take that risk.

ALEXANDRIA

Alexandria offered Archimedes the best education to be found anywhere in the Greek world. The city, founded by Alexander the Great in 332 BC, was still young when Archimedes arrived. However, Alexandria had already become the center for Greek culture and learning. When Alexander the Great died, his generals divided the empire, including all the lands he had conquered extending from Greece and Egypt all the way into India. Ptolemy took Egypt and turned Alexandria into the great center for art and learning that it was.

Ptolemy built the great Library of Alexandria. His aim was to gather into it all the known books in the world. Though that may have been an unrealistic goal, the library did contain an impressive half-million

This 1813 oil painting by Vincenzo Camuccini shows Ptolemy II founding the Library of Alexandria in Egypt. Founded in the third century BC, the Library of Alexandria was the largest repository of knowledge in the world at that time. During the rule of Ptolemy III, all visitors to the Egyptian city were required to hand over all written materials they were carrying with them to be copied by the library's scribes. This great library was eventually destroyed, resulting in a huge loss of knowledge.

books or more. Attached to the library was the Museum, which Ptolemy built in about 300 BC. The term "museum," which is still used today, literally means "place of muses." It was a place where the scholars could ponder, or think about, intellectual ideas. Many did just that, producing encyclopedias of knowledge.

Archimedes was able to study many texts at the great library and museum.

Today, scholars would consider the Museum of Alexandria a great university. The school surpassed all others of its time in science, philosophy, poetry, and music. The Museum was also rich in scientific facilities. It had observatories, consulting rooms, botanical and zoological gardens, and anatomy lecture halls, to name a few. Scientists came to this cultural center from all around the civilized world.

STUDYING EUCLID

While in Alexandria, Archimedes studied the works of Euclid, the great geometer. Euclid, who lived in Alexandria from about 330 BC to 275 BC, was also Greek. Euclid died before Archimedes was old enough to go to Alexandria, but his followers carried on his work at the Museum. Euclid was both a great mathematician and teacher. He is best known for having gathered all the mathematical theories that were known before him and tying them together with his own important work in geometry. He combined all these ideas in an ordered and logical way in his book *The Elements*. There are thirteen books of Euclid's *Elements*. Within these books are plane geometry

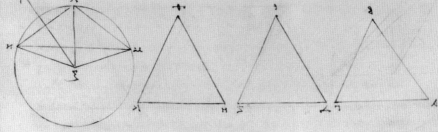

This is a manuscript page from Euclid's *Elements*, a mathematical work consisting of thirteen books. Euclid's *Elements* is, essentially, an ancient geometry textbook. He compiled all of the knowledge that existed on geometry at the time, creating a work that would influence scientists such as Galileo and Sir Isaac Newton. Euclid, who is believed to have been a student of the philosopher Plato, wrote *The Elements* in about 300 BC.

(geometry that deals with one- and two-dimensional shapes such as circles, lines, and polygons); the nature and properties of whole numbers (numbers such as 0, 1, 2, 3, and so on); solid geometry (three-dimensional solids such as spheres or cubes); and the theory of proportions and magnitude. Geometry students used *The Elements* for more than 2,000 years, and they undoubtedly had an influence on the work of Archimedes.

Archimedes at Play

Archimedes loved geometry so much that even his games involved geometrical shapes. Archimedes wrote about a game he developed called the Archimedes Box. The game was a sort of blank puzzle made up of fourteen ivory pieces. The polygon-shaped puzzle pieces fit together to form a rectangle. One of the objects of the game was to reform the rectangle after mixing up the pieces. Another popular activity was to rearrange the pieces to form other geometrical shapes, or interesting things such as elephants, trees, or boats. The Greeks called the game *stomachion*, which is believed to mean "something that drives you wild."

DEVELOPING PHILOSOPHIES

While studying in Alexandria, Egypt, Archimedes developed a taste for applied mathematics, or putting math to practical use. During the Hellenistic period, there was a difference between Egyptian and Greek mathematics. Greek mathematics was more theoretical. The Greeks sought to find the principles, or truths, of mathematics. Egyptian mathematics, however, was more practical, or useful for everyday life. Egyptian mathematicians were interested in calculations concerning land measurement, construction, and irrigation. Prior to the Hellenistic period, there were no places like Alexandria, which was influenced by both theoretical and applied mathematics. By the third century BC, the school in Alexandria was noted for such practical devices as water clocks, hydraulic devices, and machines driven by compressed air. Historians believe that Archimedes learned all about such devices while studying in Alexandria. In fact, that is where he invented his first practical device.

Plutarch, the first-century Greek biographer, wrote accounts of many famous Greeks and Romans, including Archimedes. According to Plutarch, the great mathematician Archimedes valued his theoretical work much more than his practical works. In fact,

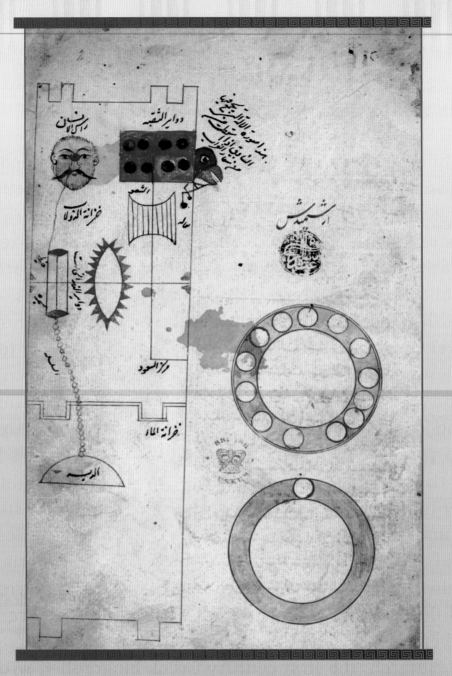

This diagram comes from a sixteenth- or seventeenth-century Arabic translation of an Archimedes manuscript called *On the Water Clock*. Although the original copy of *On the Water Clock* was lost, Arabic translations dating back to the ninth century still exist. Prior to the invention of the mechanical clock, people had been devising ways to tell time for thousands of years with varying degrees of success. The water clock Archimedes described in his manuscript would have been the most accurate clock of its time.

Plutarch wrote that Archimedes thought of applied mathematics as ignoble, or shameful, and that it was not worthy of pursuit. However, some historians believe that this may not have been true. They believe that Plutarch may have been attributing his own feelings to Archimedes.

MAKING FRIENDS

In Alexandria, Archimedes studied physics, astronomy, and mathematics with many other great minds of the time. Archimedes became lifelong friends with

Eratosthenes of Cyrene was an astronomer and poet who became close friends with Archimedes. Besides calculating the circumference of Earth, Eratosthenes is also believed to have invented the word "geography" to describe the science of measuring the physical features of Earth's surface. Eratosthenes created one of the most accurate maps of the known world during his lifetime.

two men: Conon of the Greek island of Samos, and Eratosthenes of Cyrene (now Shahhat, Libya). Conon taught mathematics to Archimedes at the Museum. Not only was Conon a gifted mathematician, but he was also one of the great early astronomers. He studied the sun's eclipses and is credited with the discovery of the constellation Coma Berenices. Archimedes respected Conon very much, both as a mathematician and as a friend. In fact, Conon was one of the greatest influences in Archimedes' life.

Archimedes' friend Eratosthenes settled in Alexandria and became the head of the famous library. Eratosthenes was the first to estimate Earth's circumference and tilt. He also calculated the sizes of the sun and the moon and their distance from Earth. Eratosthenes also became a noted geographer. As such, he was the first to indicate longitude and latitude on a map.

For the rest of his life, Archimedes corresponded with these men, exchanging ideas. In fact, some of Archimedes' finest work is found in letters to Conon. After Conon's death, Archimedes corresponded with one of Conon's pupils, Dositheus. With these three men, Archimedes discussed many problems and their solutions.

After studying in Alexandria, Archimedes returned home to his beloved Syracuse, where it is believed he spent the rest of his life. However, his studies in Alexandria became the foundation on which he built his career as a scientist and mathematician. He went on to discover many monumental things in both theoretical and applied mathematics.

Archimedes wrote about his findings in various papers called treatises. Of the treatises he wrote, only ten have survived. In his most recently discovered treatise, *The Method*, Archimedes describes the process of his discovery of mathematical truths. In this treatise, discovered in 1906, Archimedes explains how he first designed a way to attack a problem, then masterfully organized a plan, then sternly eliminated everything that was not immediately relevant to his purpose, and then, finally, finished the work. Archimedes wrote many treatises about his findings. Some of these are on display in museums today. Archimedes' surviving treatises are mathematical works of art, and it is unfortunate that many more have been lost.

3 ARCHIMEDES AND THEORETICAL MATHEMATICS

The word mathematics comes from the Greek word *mathema*, which means "lesson." Theoretical mathematics is a type of mathematics that is concerned more with mathematical theory than it is with practical applications of mathematics. Archimedes was very fond of theoretical, or pure, mathematics— mathematics without the immediate consideration of direct applications. He worked with arithmetic, which is the study of numbers; trigonometry, which calculates the relationship between distances and directions; and geometry, which analyzes the nature and properties of shapes.

Archimedes proved to be a very modern thinker. Of all the ancients, Archimedes had the greatest freedom of his contemporaries in his exploration of mathematics.

This was due to the stature, strength, and leisure time that came with being born into a higher social class.

Many other ancient mathematicians were restricted to philosophical rules set forth by Plato. Plato, a philosopher who died sixty years before Archimedes' birth, believed that the study of geometry required only a straightedge and a pair of compasses. He considered any understanding reached with the use of other tools to be vulgar. Today, freedom to explore different ideas is a privilege that some mathematicians may take for granted. This freedom, however, was hard-won by centuries of previous mathematicians.

Archimedes spent most of his time contemplating new problems to solve. He drew geometric figures in the dirt and even in the ashes of extinguished fires. His freedom to explore mathematics resulted in some very bold discoveries that were far beyond his time. He invented his own counting system and developed new ways to calculate the areas and volumes of geometric figures. Some of his mathematical methods closely resembled integral calculus, a very complicated branch of mathematics discovered 2,000 years later. In fact, Archimedes' work with theoretical mathematics cleared up almost every geometric measuring problem that was left to be solved during his time.

ARCHIMEDES' WORK WITH CIRCLES

Archimedes conducted many studies of the circle. It was important to him to find an accurate way to calculate the area of this shape. One way to do this is to make use of the ratio between the circumference (the distance around the circle) and the diameter (the length of a straight line stretching from one side of the circle to the other, and passing through the circle's center). This ratio, known as pi, is represented by the symbol π.

Pi got its name because it is the first letter of the Greek word *perimetros* (perimeter or circumference). The area of a circle can be calculated easily once the diameter is measured. The problem was that ancient mathematicians did not have an accurate value for pi. Archimedes sought to fix that.

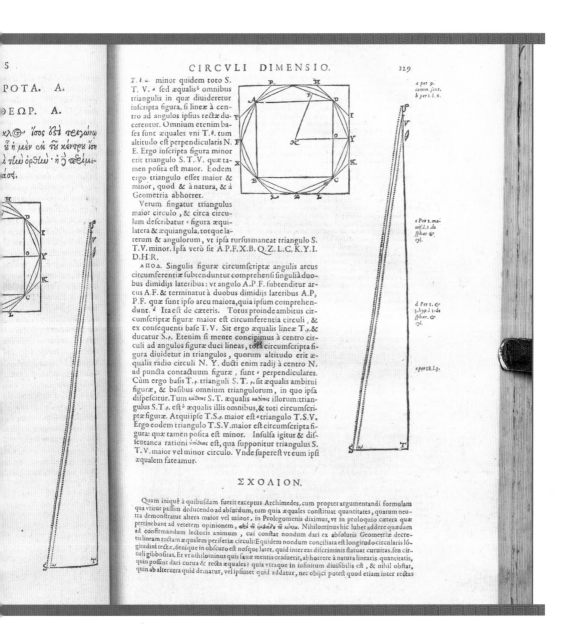

This 1615 Latin translation of Archimedes' complete works was made by David Rivault. This translation, which also contains the original Greek text, reintroduced the works of Archimedes to mathematicians in the seventeenth century.

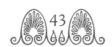

Prior to Archimedes' work, the best value for pi came from the Egyptians. They calculated it to be 3.16. However, that, and all other values of pi known before it, had been an estimate based on measurements. Archimedes would be the first to calculate the value mathematically.

Archimedes described his work with circles in his treatise *Measurement of the Circle.* In it, he describes how he used two polygons (figures with three or more sides) to find an approximation for pi. Archimedes drew one of the polygons just inside the circle and one just outside the circle. The perimeter of the circle would lie somewhere between the perimeters of the two polygons.

Archimedes then measured the length of the polygons' perimeters. By increasing the number of sides that the polygons had, Archimedes was able to bring the perimeters of the polygons closer to the circumference of the circle. Archimedes began with six-sided polygons, which touched the circle at six points each. He then increased this number to twelve, then to twenty-four, and so on. In order to have enough points on the polygons so that every one of their points corresponded to a point on the circle, Archimedes would have had to continue increasing the number of sides endlessly. This is because there are an infinite number of points on a circle. That means that there is no end to the number of points. Archimedes would have had to increase the number of sides of his polygons forever!

Many ancient mathematicians did not believe that infinity was truly infinite. They believed that with enough hard work and patience, infinity could be reached. Archimedes did not share this belief, however. He knew that infinity was uncountable, beyond reach. Therefore, he stopped adding sides to his polygons when they had ninety-six sides each. He then found the perimeter of the inside polygon, as well as that for the one on the outside—no easy task in Archimedes' day. In this way, Archimedes calculated pi to be between the values of $3\frac{10}{71}$ and $3\frac{1}{7}$. As decimals, these numbers are about 3.141 and 3.143, respectively. Archimedes' value for pi was correct to two decimal places. Later mathematicians gradually improved on Archimedes' figure by using polygons with more and more sides so that they more closely fit the shape of a circle. Today, the value of pi is calculated to be 3.14159~, or rounded off to 3.142.

EXPRESSION OF LARGE NUMBERS

One of Archimedes' great contributions to mathematics was that he eliminated the fear of using

The Unending Number

Ludolph van Ceulen was a Dutchman who, in 1610, completed a calculation for pi based on a polygon with more than 30 billion sides. As you can imagine, this calculation occupied him for much of his life, and he worked on it almost to his dying day. It did, however, establish the value of pi to thirty-five decimal places. He was rewarded by having the number inscribed on his tombstone. In Germany, the number is also called the Ludolphine number, named after him.

ATHEN. BAT. LIB. II.   343

LUDOLPHUS A COLLEN
MATHESEOS BELGICUS PROFESS.

LVDOL-

Ludolph van Ceulen was the first person to calculate pi to thirty-five decimal places. In Germany, pi was called the Ludolphine number for many years in honor of his achievement. Although it is believed that he never received a university education, Van Ceulen spent much of his adult life teaching mathematics.

In 1961, more than 350 years after Van Ceulen's calculation, a computer calculated the value of pi to 100,000 places in just eight hours. In 1981, in Japan, a computer took only a little more than five days to calculate the value of pi to 2 million decimal places. Imagine how upset Ludolph van Ceulen would be if he knew that!

No matter how many more decimal places or how much faster we are able to calculate the value of pi, there will never be an end. The number goes on and on infinitely.

large numbers. Not only did many ancient Greeks not believe in infinity, they only counted up to 10,000, what they called a myriad. They also believed that no number existed that was high enough to count the number of grains of sand it would take to fill the universe. In those days, people thought the universe was the space between the sun, the moon, and the five planets known at that time: Venus, Mercury, Mars, Jupiter, and Saturn. Since no one could actually sit down and count the sand, they assumed that the number must have been so high that it did not exist. In his short book *The Sand*

Reckoner, addressed to King Gelon of Syracuse, Archimedes wrote:

> Many people believe, King Gelon, that the grains of sand are infinite in multitude; and I mean by the sand not only that which exists around Syracuse and the rest of Sicily, but also that which is found in every region, whether inhabited or uninhabited. Others think that although their number is not without limit, no number can ever be named which will be greater than the number of grains of sand. But I shall try to prove to you that among the numbers which I have named there are those which exceed the number of grains in a heap of sand the size not only of the earth, but even of the universe.

Archimedes loved a challenge, so he decided to try to count the sand needed to fill the universe. To show that he was not being easy on himself, he chose a very fine sand to fill the universe. First, Archimedes counted the number of grains of sand that would form a cluster the size of a poppy seed. He figured that one poppy would not contain more than 10,000 grains of

A Matter of Revenge

Around the time that Archimedes was studying in Alexandria, another young man was also there. His name was Apollonius. Apollonius worked with conics—the curves you get when you slice a cone. Today, Apollonius is known for naming these curves: ellipse, parabola, and hyperbola.

Though Archimedes and Apollonius may not have met, they were certainly familiar with one another's work. Some historians believe that Apollonius rubbed Archimedes the wrong way. Apparently, Apollonius tried to outdo some of Archimedes' achievements. Historians believe that Apollonius annoyed Archimedes so much that Archimedes challenged the young scientist with an extremely difficult problem.

Archimedes' problem is known today as "the cattle problem." In the problem, Helios, the sun god, had a herd of bulls and cows. Some of them were yellow, some white, some black, and some spotted. Archimedes established seven relationships between the number of each color and the sex. For example, he said that the number of white cows was $7/12$ of the number of all the black cows and bulls together.

In addition to the seven relationships, there were also two special requirements. The first requirement was that the yellow and spotted bulls grouped together had to form a triangular shape. Second, the black and white bulls, when grouped together, had to form a square. The challenge of the problem was to figure out how many cattle there were.

Most historians doubt whether either Archimedes or Apollonius actually ever solved the problem. In fact, it took more than 2,000 years and the fastest computers to solve it. Though the question itself is simple, the solution is actually quite complicated. It turns out that the smallest possible answer for the herd's total size is a 206,545-digit number. Now that's a lot of cattle!

sand. Next, he counted the number of poppy seeds that would equal the size of a man's finger. Then, he calculated how many fingers it would take to fill a stadium. Archimedes continued in this way until he had his answer. In *The Sand Reckoner*, Archimedes estimated the number of grains of sand needed to fill the universe to be less than 10^{63} (that is, 1 followed by sixty-three zeros). Today, calculations using a sphere with the radius of Pluto's orbit puts the number of grains of sand needed to fill our universe at about 10^{51}.

In order to convey his very large number, Archimedes had to develop his own numbering system, as numbers did not exist to count that high during the third century BC. Using his system, Archimedes was capable of expressing, in language, numbers up to

1 followed by 80,000 million million zeros. Archimedes noted in *The Sand Reckoner* that even though this number is larger than any number the Greeks had seen before, it still did not come close to infinity.

Though Archimedes' number system never caught on, it did serve to show that tremendously large numbers can be formed by multiplying smaller numbers together over and over. Today, we use a number system called exponential notation to describe large numbers. This system multiplies tens together to get larger numbers. For instance 10^2 means 10 x 10, or 100. Here, ten is called the base number and two is called the exponent. Likewise 10^5, or 10 to the fifth power, is 10 x 10 x 10 x 10 x 10, or 100,000. We most likely owe this modern, much simpler, system of expressing numbers to Archimedes.

THE METHOD OF EXHAUSTION

Archimedes especially loved geometry. Some of the geometrical problems that Archimedes solved concerned the areas and volumes of geometric figures, both plane and solid. Plane figures are two-dimensional and flat, having the dimensions of length and width. Plane figures can be drawn on paper. In addition to

One of ancient Greece's astronomers and geometers, Apollonius of Perga (circa 262–190 BC), produced a number of mathematical works. Unfortunately, only two of his works survive. The first, entitled *Cutting Off of a Ratio*, survives only in an Arabic translation. His major work, *Conics*, originally published as eight books, also survives—although one of the books is lost. This edition of *Conics* was printed in 1710.

Ariſtippus Philoſophus Socraticus, naufragio cum ejectus ad Rhodienſium litus animadvertiſſet Geometrica ſchemata deſcripta, exclamaviſſe ad comites ita dicitur, Bene ſperemus, Hominum enim veſtigia video.
Vitruv. Architect. lib.6.Præf.

delin. M.Burghers ſculpt Univ. Oxon.

APOLLONII PERGÆI
CONICORUM
LIBRI OCTO,

ET

SERENI ANTISSENSIS
DE SECTIONE
CYLINDRI & CONI
LIBRI DUO.

delin.Burghers sculp.Oxon Ox.1704

OXONIÆ,

E THEATRO SHELDONIANO, An. Dom. MDCCX.

studying the circle, Archimedes also studied plane figures like triangles, spirals, parabolas, and ellipses. He wrote about these in his treatises *Measurement of the Circle*, *Quadrature of the Parabola*, and *On Spirals*.

Solid figures are three-dimensional (having the dimensions of length, width, and height) and take up space. Some examples of the solid figures that Archimedes studied are spheres, cylinders, and cones. He recorded his work with solids in his writings *On the Sphere and Cylinder* and *On Conoids and Spheroids*.

Archimedes devised new ways to determine the formulas for the areas and volumes of these and other plane and solid figures. One of the new strategies he used was called the method of exhaustion. This method was an early form of integration, a type of calculus. To determine the areas of sections

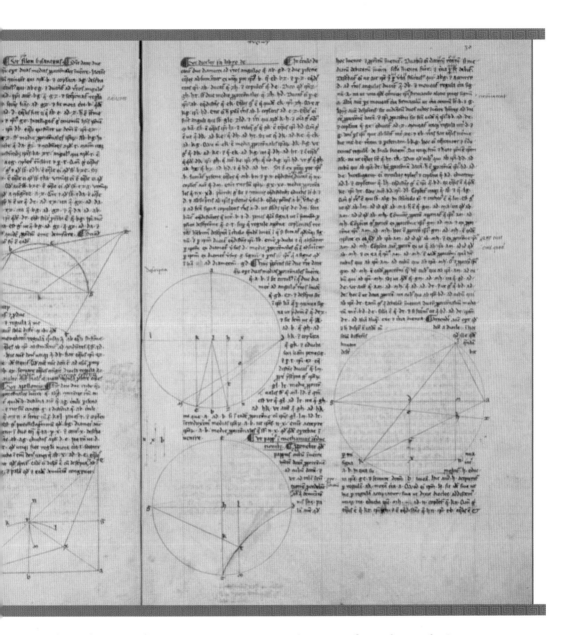

This thirteenth-century Latin translation of Archimedes' manuscript *On the Sphere and the Cylinder* was made by William of Moerbeke. The translation also includes commentary from the mathematician named Eutocius, who lived during the sixth century.

bound by geometric figures, such as parabolas and ellipses, Archimedes broke the sections into smaller and smaller areas and then added the areas together. Archimedes used the method of exhaustion to find his value for pi. Archimedes elaborated on the method of exhaustion in his treatise *The Method*. Amazingly, this anticipated the development of an extremely complex form of mathematics called integral calculus by 2,000 years!

Archimedes was a great problem solver. Many historians, including Plutarch, describe him as one of the greatest mechanical geniuses of all time because of his application of mathematics to his inventions. However, many believe that Archimedes had a great contempt for those inventions. He preferred to associate himself with his theoretical achievements. In fact, many of Archimedes' inventions began as experiments that he conducted in order to prove his theories.

Archimedes also solved many practical problems for King Hiero, with whom he had a close, personal relationship. Some of Archimedes' best discoveries, such as the behavior of water, came to him while helping the king. Requests from the king also resulted in inventions such as pulleys and levers that could move tremendous weights and astonishing arrays of war machines, such as cranes, and catapult-like missile launchers. Though Archimedes may have had disdain for his practical inventions, he certainly did make a name for himself in the field of applied mathematics.

ARCHIMEDEAN SCREW

While he was studying in Alexandria, Egypt, Archimedes is said to have discovered a very useful and practical tool, a device now known as the Archimedean screw. This invention was used as a means of pumping water out of the Nile River. The Nile, which flows through Egypt, is the longest river in the world. Every year, the Nile overflowed, giving the land around it plenty of water for the Egyptian farmers to grow their crops. However, during times when there was no rain, the farmers had trouble watering their fields. In order to irrigate their fields, the Egyptians had to carry water in buckets from the river. Watering their fields in this way took a lot of time and effort. Archimedes' screw, however, made their lives a whole lot easier.

The Archimedean screw is a hollow tube, or cylinder, that is open at each end. Inside the cylinder is a continuous screw that forms spiral chambers. It works when one end of the screw is placed in the water and

This 1958 woodcut by Peter Flotner shows the Archimedean screw. This screw was the first machine that Archimedes invented, and it is still in use today. The Archimedean screw works by pushing water upward from a lower water source. This farmer (*inset*) uses the screw to irrigate his crops.

the other end is turned. The turning motion pushes the water into the spiral chambers, forcing it to flow upward, from one chamber to the next until it finally spills out the top and onto the land.

Some Egyptian farmers are still using the Archimedean screw to irrigate their fields. It ranges in size from a quarter of an inch to 12 feet (0.6 centimeters to 3.7 meters) in diameter. The screw is also used in the Netherlands, as well as in other countries, where unwanted water needs to be drained from the surface of the land. It forces the water from the land, into the spiral chambers, and finally back into the canals.

In Archimedes' day, his invention was used mostly for irrigation. But there were other uses as well—seamen used the screw to bail water out of their ships. The Archimedean screw is still widely used today, and many modern inventions are based on the design and principle behind it. Motorboat and airplane propellers are quite similar to the Archimedean screw. Motorboat propellers push water through the propeller behind them, driving the boat forward. Airplane propellers, called air screws, move planes forward by pushing air backward. The Archimedean screw may have been the first machine that Archimedes invented, but it was not the last.

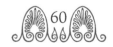

ARCHIMEDES' COMPOUND PULLEY

Archimedes wrote about what is called theoretical mechanics. Theoretical mechanics is the in-depth description and explanation of the motion of objects in the universe. It was with theoretical mechanics that Archimedes solved the problem of moving a large

This image, taken from an 1824 issue of *Mechanic's Magazine*, shows Archimedes using a lever to lift the world. Archimedes did not invent the lever, but he did work out the mathematical laws governing its use. Archimedes would apply these laws to the design of a number of practical inventions later in his life.

weight with a small amount of force. This is done by means of what is called a compound pulley.

A pulley is a machine consisting of a rope wrapped around a wheel. This machine can turn or reverse the direction of a force. Compound pulleys use two or more pulleys to divide the amount of force needed to perform a task.

This 1876 woodcut depicts one of Archimedes' inventions being used to move a large ship. Archimedes designed intricate pulley systems that easily moved ships and other heavy objects. He is considered to be the first mathematical physicist.

Compound pulleys are such useful machines that they are still used today. If you walk into an auto mechanic's garage, you might see a large compound pulley used to lift the engines out of cars. Compound pulleys are also used at construction sites to lift heavy amounts of building material. These machines haven't changed much since Archimedes' day.

Archimedes declared to King Hiero that any amount of weight could be moved by any amount of force, no matter how small. Even a great weight could be moved with just a small force. He even boasted to the king, as quoted by the mathematician Pappus of Alexandria, "Give me a place to stand, and I will move the world."

Though Archimedes greatly valued pure, mathematical reasoning, it seems that King Hiero felt that mathematical theories were nothing until applied to practical things. To prove his statement to Hiero, Archimedes filled one of the king's large ships with many passengers and cargo. He then sat far away and effortlessly moved the ship through the water by simply pulling on the end of a compound pulley.

Archimedes based the design for his ship-moving device on the lever and fulcrum. Levers are machines that reduce the amount of force needed to do work by spreading the force over a greater distance. Called simple machines, levers have only two parts: the handle and the fulcrum. The handle is the part that is pushed or pulled, and the fulcrum is the point on which the lever turns or balances. A pulley is a type of lever. A fork is another example of a lever, the fulcrum being the point at which your fingers hold it. Scissors are an example of two levers put together. Archimedes described his work with levers in his treatise *On the Equilibrium of Planes*.

The account of Archimedes moving the ship with his compound pulley system first appeared in written form nearly 300 years after the incident occurred. For this reason, many historians believe that the story could have changed over time or been exaggerated with the telling and retelling. However, most scientists believe that in order for Archimedes to move a large ship filled with cargo and passengers, he must have used a fairly complex pulley system. Archimedes may have even used some of his other inventions in the process, including the windlass (a simple crank-and-axle arrangement used commonly to raise a bucket from a well) or the worm gear (a device in which a screwlike "worm" meshes with the teeth of a gear). These inventions attached to a compound pulley, scientists agree, could have gotten the job done.

THE LAW OF BUOYANCY

After coming to power, Hiero wished to present his favorite temple with a gift, a golden *stephane*. Similar to a crown, stephanes were often seen on the statues of Greek goddesses. Hiero ordered a goldsmith to make one out of pure gold. However, when the crown was finished, Hiero suspected that the goldsmith had mixed the gold with a less valuable metal, such as silver.

As he so often did when faced with a difficult problem, Hiero turned to Archimedes for a solution. Historians are not exactly sure how Archimedes went about testing the king's crown. He had surely thought of a way to test it without damaging it, but there are probably several ways he could have completed the task. As with most of his practical ideas, Archimedes failed to write down what he did.

The story of how Archimedes solved this problem was first recorded two or three centuries after Archimedes' time. It was first mentioned in a book about architecture that was published in about 30 BC by the Roman architect Vitruvius. As the story goes, Archimedes' inspiration came while he was taking a bath. As he was getting into the tub, he noticed that water spilled over the sides of the tub as he submerged

Augenscheinliche Figur der geschwinden erfindung
Archimedis.

By realizing that his body displaced water in his bath, Archimedes inadvertently discovered the laws of density and buoyancy. The law of buoyancy, also known as Archimedes' principle, states that the force of buoyancy acting on an object is equal to the weight of the fluid the object displaces.

himself. Upon further experimentation, he realized that anything immersed in the tub would displace a volume of water that was equal to its own volume (volume is the amount of space that an object occupies). Archimedes also realized that when samples of two different materials weighed the same, the denser material displaced less water than the less dense material. Density is the mass contained within a unit volume.

If two objects weigh the same, the denser material would take up less volume than the less dense material. All Archimedes needed to do to solve the king's problem was to compare the amount of water displaced by the crown to the amount of water displaced by pure gold of equal weight. According to the story, Archimedes was so excited by his discovery that he jumped from the bath, forgetting to clothe himself, and ran naked through the streets of Syracuse shouting, "Eureka!" meaning, "I have found it!"

Vitruvius states that Archimedes obtained a block of gold and a block of silver that weighed the same as the crown. He then compared the volumes of the three objects (the gold, the silver, and the crown). Archimedes did this by filling a jug to the brim with water, dropping each object, in turn, into the jug, and carefully measuring how much water each object displaced. Gold is denser than silver. Therefore, a sample of gold would displace less water than a sample of silver that weighs the same amount. In the same way, the sample of pure gold would displace a smaller volume of water than an impure crown. If the crown were made of pure gold, it would displace the same amount of water as the block of pure gold.

Upon doing his experiment, Archimedes saw that the block of pure gold displaced less water than the crown. This meant that the crown was less dense than the gold and was not pure. Indeed, the king had been cheated.

Though the fate of the goldsmith is unknown, what is far more important is what Archimedes had done. He had made a discovery that would lead to the founding of the science of hydrostatics. The word "hydrostatics" comes from the Greek words *hydro*, meaning "water," and *statikos*, meaning "causing to stand." The science of hydrostatics deals with the laws that govern how liquids behave when they are at rest, or not moving. Archimedes was so far ahead of his time with the concept of hydrostatics that it was not until the 1800s that any new discoveries were made in this field.

From his bathtub experience, Archimedes came to understand the law of buoyancy. He described his findings in a treatise entitled *On Floating Bodies*. Buoyancy is the name for the upward lifting force of water. Today, this law is known as Archimedes' principle. Archimedes' principle states that when an object is placed in a fluid, it is buoyed up by a force that is equal to the weight of the fluid it displaces. Let's say that Archimedes' body took the place of about 2 cubic feet (0.05 cubic meters) of water when he

submerged himself in his bath. Therefore, his body would have been buoyed up by a force equal to the weight of 2 cubic feet (0.05 cu m) of water.

Archimedes is also credited with the idea of specific gravity. Before Archimedes, scientists were not quite sure how to accurately compare the densities of different objects. Specific gravity accomplishes this. Specific gravity is the weight of an object relative to water. For example, gold is nineteen times as heavy as an equal volume of water, so its specific gravity is nineteen. Silver has a specific gravity of eleven. Archimedes found the idea of specific gravity very useful when he was talking about buoyancy. He showed that anything with a specific gravity less than one would float in water, while anything with a specific gravity greater than one would sink. Based on those findings, it is safe to say that no matter whether Hiero's crown was made of silver or gold, it would have definitely sunk.

CENTERS OF GRAVITY

Gravity is the force that pulls objects toward Earth. Gravity also pulls two objects together. Most scientists agree that the first real understanding of gravity came during the seventeenth century with Sir Isaac

This translation of Archimedes' *On Floating Bodies* dates back to the tenth century. Since much of Archimedes' work was destroyed, much of it only exists in translation. Before the invention of printing presses, books were copied by hand. As you might imagine, copying a book took a very long time. There were usually only a very few fragile copies made of each book. If these copies were destroyed, their contents were lost.

Newton. However, 2,000 years before Newton, Greek scientists already had a faint idea about gravity and its effects here on Earth. Archimedes experimented with equilibrium, or balance, and centers of gravity for both solid and plane figures. His studies on centers of gravity, explained in his treatise *On the Equilibrium of Planes*, formed the foundation for the science of theoretical mechanics.

Gravity was discovered by the scientist Sir Isaac Newton (1642–1727). As legend has it, Newton observed an apple falling from a tree, which led him to outline the law of universal gravitation. Newton also set down the laws of motion and pioneered the mathematical techniques of calculus.

Archimedes began his investigation of the center of gravity with the lever. The basic law of the lever may have been known before Archimedes' time, but he was the first to prove it. Imagine a seesaw, which is the simplest type of lever. Archimedes assumed that equal weights at equal but opposite distances from the fulcrum of such a lever will balance. Equal weights at unequal distances, however, will not balance. In that case, the weight that is farther from the fulcrum will tilt its side of the lever down. Archimedes also assumed

Mobiles

Archimedes' discovery about levers was later applied to such things as weight-lifting equipment and seesaws. You can study what Archimedes learned about levers by making a mobile. Making a mobile is an easy way to learn about centers of gravity. As you know, when you make a mobile, you use sticks, some thread, a ruler, and some small objects. Each mobile is a lever in equilibrium. When you make a mobile, you have to spend time finding the right positions to hang the objects so that the mobile is evenly balanced. You can make your mobile as simple or as fancy as you wish. You just have to use the principles Archimedes discovered.

that if the two weights balance and additional weight is added to one of the sides, the side on which the additional weight is added will go down. Likewise, if the two weights are even and weight is taken away from one side, the side holding the weight that is not changed will go down.

From balancing weights against one another like this, Archimedes moved on to balancing parts of objects. By doing this, he was able to find the balancing point, or center of gravity, for many different shapes. All objects will balance on their center of gravity. For some shapes, the center of gravity is obvious. For a circle, the center of gravity is its center. However, Archimedes proved that an object's center of gravity is not always its center. If an object has a heavy end and a light end, the center of gravity will lie closer to the heavy end.

A spoon is a good example of this. If you were to balance a spoon on your finger, you would have to place your finger closer to the head of the spoon (the heavy end). The point on the spoon on which it would balance on your finger is its center of gravity.

Archimedes showed that the center of gravity for a square or a rectangle is the point at which lines drawn between the corners cross. A triangle's center of gravity is found by drawing lines from each corner to the center of the opposite side. The center of gravity is the point at which the lines cross. Archimedes also found the centers of gravity for more complicated shapes. One example of a complicated shape for which he found the center of gravity is a segment of a parabola. A parabola is a curve, and a segment of a parabola is the shape that would be made if the parabola was cut off by a straight line.

WARTIME INVENTIONS

The people of Syracuse wondered how long it would be before Rome and Carthage would battle for control of Syracuse. In order to protect his city, King Hiero signed a treaty with the Romans, pledging friendship and cooperation. In return, the Romans offered protection from the Carthaginians. Hiero wondered, however, how much help the Romans would actually provide in the event of an attack. Not wanting to find out, he turned, as he so often did when presented with a problem, to his trusted friend Archimedes. Archimedes agreed to use his expertise to help Hiero devise a defense system for Syracuse. Though Archimedes had concentrated on mathematics rather than inventing practical machines, especially those meant for destruction, he saw the need to protect the city he loved and had called home for so many years.

This fresco by Italian artist Giulio Parigi depicts the claw of Archimedes. One of the most infamous devices Archimedes ever invented, this war machine consisted of a crane and a grappling hook. The grappling hook would latch on to the bottom of an enemy ship, and the lever action of the crane would capsize it.

Among the machines he designed for the protection of the city were catapults that could hurl heavy stones over the city's walls. These catapults were constructed so ingeniously that they were equally effective at both long and short ranges. Archimedes also designed weapons that discharged showers of missiles through holes in the city walls.

Some of Archimedes' other inventions consisted of long, movable poles that projected beyond the city walls. These could either drop heavy weights on the enemy's ships or grab them with an iron hand or beak-like crane. The iron claws, which were controlled by ropes and other mechanisms, could destabilize or capsize an enemy ship. Once the sailors had fallen overboard, the claw could then release the ship. It was also said that Archimedes developed a way to use mirrors to magnify the sun's heat onto enemy ships, causing them to catch fire. Modern-day experiments have shown that this would prove to be very difficult to accomplish, however. Many historians regard Archimedes' use of mirrors as nothing more than a legend.

Hiero was quite pleased with all of Archimedes' weapons. The king ordered that they be kept at the ready in the event of an emergency. When Hiero died around 215 BC, the machines were in perfect working order, but they had yet to be used.

The last years of Archimedes' life were anything but uneventful. When he was a young man, the First Punic War (264–241 BC) had ended with a peace treaty between Rome and Carthage. Although the two enemies had signed a treaty, the conflict was not over, and both sides knew it. The treaty had left the Carthaginians in an impossible position— they had to choose whether to fight to regain their position or simply fade into insignificance. The Carthaginians' unwillingness to sit back and do nothing, along with the Romans' continued aggressiveness, led the people of Carthage to the decision to fight.

In 218 BC, the Romans and the Carthaginians renewed their fighting, marking the start of the Second Punic War. At that

This 1521 painting depicts the Battle of Zama in the Second Punic War. Hannibal was an extremely accomplished military leader, who is famous for using elephants to cross the Alps during the Second Punic War. Elephants were occasionally used during warfare at that time to break an opponent's ranks and trample enemy soldiers.

time, Hannibal, a military genius who had a lifelong disdain for Rome, led the Carthaginian troops. Under Hannibal's leadership, Carthage won the first round of battles against Rome. Although Hannibal's success was shortlived, it was enough to convince many Syracusans that they had formed an alliance with the wrong side.

WAR WITH ROME

By 215 BC, the Second Punic War was in full swing. Rome and Carthage were fighting and Syracuse lay near the path of the Roman fleet. Hiero had honored his treaty with Rome while he lived. However, upon his death in

Archimedes invented many weapons during his lifetime. He was rumored to have invented large mirrors that focused the light of the sun on Roman leader Marcellus's ships and set them on fire. Modern-day investigations have discovered that this would be an extremely difficult feat to accomplish, and it probably never happened.

215 BC, his fifteen-year-old grandson Hieronymus became ruler of Sicily. Hieronymus broke Syracuse's treaty with Rome and formed an alliance with Carthage. Alarmed by Syracuse's betrayal, Rome quickly turned its attention toward the great city. The Roman leader Marcellus anticipated a speedy victory over the Syracusans. However, this was not the case. The Syracusans were ready for the fight, thanks to Archimedes, who had, at King Hiero's request, used his knowledge of mathematics to build great weapons.

It was time for Archimedes to prepare the war machines for action. As the machines had been kept in working order, none needed repair—they were ready to go.

When the Romans arrived, the Syracusans awaited them with Archimedes' inventions. The Romans attacked with a full frontal assault from both land and sea. However, they were no match for Archimedes' inventions. Archimedes' super-catapults hurled stones, each weighing more than a quarter of a ton. They demolished Marcellus's small catapults and mowed down his land forces. The cranelike beaks and iron claws reached down over the walls of the city, seized Marcellus's approaching ships, and sank or shattered them. The Romans tried for two years to

This statue of Marcellus shows the Roman general as a young man. Although Marcellus did not harm the civilian inhabitants of Syracuse, he carted off their art treasures, installing them in Rome. As a military leader, Marcellus was very impressed with Archimedes' war machines.

capture Syracuse, but with no luck. Without victory in sight, Marcellus backed down. The Roman troops so feared Archimedes' inventions that if the Syracusans so much as dangled a rope over the city wall, the Romans recoiled in terror for fear that Archimedes was setting one of his inventions down on them.

Marcellus, however, was no fool. He ceased further plans for frontal attacks of Syracuse. He decided

instead to attack Syracuse from behind. With great patience, Marcellus waited for his chance. His opportunity came while the Syracusans were celebrating a religious festival in honor of Artemis, the Greek goddess of the hunt. The Syracusans ate and drank so much at their celebration that they forgot to keep a sharp lookout. Marcellus noticed that one section of the city wall had little protection. He seized his opportunity, attacking the surprised and drunken people of Syracuse. Marcellus captured the city.

ARCHIMEDES' DEATH

Marcellus had great respect for Archimedes. Upon taking the city, the Roman general immediately sent soldiers to find the mathematician responsible for the formidable weapons. Marcellus ordered his troops not to harm Archimedes.

When the Romans began looting the city, Archimedes was alone, involved in trying to solve a mathematical problem. According to historians, Archimedes was a man capable of an intense amount of concentration. Oftentimes, when working on a problem, Archimedes concentrated so hard that he was oblivious to anything else going on around him. Archimedes did not sleep when concentrating on a problem, and he often left meals untouched until he was finished with his work.

Many times, Archimedes' servants had to drag him to his bath against his will so that they could bathe him and anoint him with oil. All the while, Archimedes would be drawing geometrical figures on any surface he could find, including his own oil-slicked body. Archimedes' inattention to dress while working through a problem was demonstrated by the story of how he ran naked through the streets of Syracuse following his discovery of the law of buoyancy. If nothing else, these examples demonstrate Archimedes' great passion for mathematics. Unfortunately, this passion may have cost Archimedes his life.

Most of the facts that we know about Archimedes' life come from a biography about the Roman leader Marcellus, which was written by the Roman biographer Plutarch. Plutarch chronicles the events of the Second Punic War, including Marcellus's struggle against the Syracusans and a lengthy section on Archimedes and his war machines. According to Plutarch, Archimedes was so deep in thought that he was unaware the city was being looted by the Romans. He did not hear the shouting, the yells, or the blasting trumpets as the Romans swept through the city. He may not have even noticed the Roman soldier who

The historian and writer Plutarch (circa AD 46–120) was extremely prolific, and many of his writings still survive today. He is known for a work called *Parallel Lives*, which contains a number of biographies of historical figures of the time. Plutarch also produced dozens of speeches and essays, which are collected in a work called *Moralia*.

PLUTARCH.

approached him as he drew diagrams in the dirt. Plutarch relates some of the oral accounts on the death of Archimedes. In one account, the soldier stepped on his diagram, angering Archimedes who snapped, "Don't disturb my circles!" Another story states that Archimedes refused to obey the soldier's orders to accompany him to Marcellus until he had finished working out his problem. In any event, the Roman soldier was so enraged that he took out his sword and killed the seventy-five-year-old mathematician.

Marcellus was deeply grieved when he heard of Archimedes' death. It is believed he ordered the execution of the soldier, stating that he was a common murderer. Marcellus made sure that Archimedes

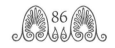

was buried with honors. He also made sure that, as Archimedes had wished, Archimedes' tombstone bore the image of a sphere within a cylinder. This image represented Archimedes' proud discovery that the volume of a sphere is two-thirds the volume of the smallest cylinder that encloses it, and that the surface of the sphere is also two-thirds the surface area of the cylinder. For example, a cylinder that just contains a sphere filled with 4 gallons (15 liters) of water is able to hold 6 gallons (23 l) of water. Archimedes regarded this as his greatest discovery.

Archimedes was obviously proud of this achievement, and indeed, he should have been. To figure out that ratio today, a mathematician would use calculus, a very advanced form of mathematics, first discovered during the seventeenth century by Sir Isaac Newton and Gottfried Leibniz. However, Archimedes' technique so resembles calculus that he shares some of the credit for its discovery.

Following Archimedes' death, mathematical progress went into a decline. Archimedes' advancements in the field of mathematics made it nearly impossible for further progress to be made until new systems, such as algebra and analytical geometry, were developed. This would not happen until seventeen centuries later.

Marcellus was greatly interested in Archimedes and ordered him to be captured alive, but the great mathematician was killed by a Roman soldier. This act ended the life of one of the greatest mathematicians that the world has ever known. Before his death, Archimedes had requested that his tombstone be inscribed with an image of one of his mathematical discoveries.

ARCHIMEDES' REDISCOVERY

Following the defeat of Syracuse by Marcellus, the city became an outpost for the growing Roman Empire. Though the Romans had overtaken the city, they left Syracuse intact. The city fared far better than Carthage, which was destroyed by the Romans during the Third Punic War (149–146 BC). In fact, Syracuse became the headquarters for the Roman

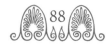

This 1781 painting by Thomas Christian Winck is entitled *Cicero Discovers the Grave of Archimedes*. Cicero (106–43 BC) was one of the greatest Roman statesmen, and he found the grave of Archimedes during a trip to Sicily in 75 BC.

government of Sicily and remained such for centuries to come. Undoubtedly, Syracuse's governmental ties to Rome brought Cicero, a lawyer and politician, to the city more than a century after Archimedes' death.

While in Syracuse, Cicero searched for Archimedes' tomb and found it in a neglected state. Cicero wrote that the tomb was easy to recognize as Archimedes' because of its engraving of a sphere within a cylinder. In 75 BC, Cicero had Archimedes' tomb restored. However, the tomb has since

disappeared, and no one knows where Archimedes is buried now. Cicero also reported seeing a planetarium in Syracuse. According to Cicero, Archimedes built the planetarium, which showed the motion of the sun, the moon, and the five known planets. During Cicero's time, the planetarium was considered to be one of Archimedes' finest achievements. It was so accurate that it could show the phases of the moon and predict the eclipses of the sun and the moon.

Archimedes had hoped that his work would help those who followed him to discover more about mathematical relationships. However, in the decades following his death, Archimedes' influence was minimal. Historians suggest that this may have been due to the domination of the Roman Empire. The Greeks loved theoretical, abstract science, but the practical Romans had little interest in theoretical works, particularly mathematics. Only a few of Archimedes' ideas gained prominence—those that were relatively easy to understand and communicate. One such discovery was the approximate value of pi, which became a standard mathematical notation during Roman times.

For the most part, Archimedes' work was lost to the West for centuries. Some of the credit for Archimedes'

The Monk Who Ran Out of Paper

The rediscovery of Archimedes continues even into the present day. One of Archimedes' treatises, *The Method*, was found fairly recently, in 1906. Although this work had been mentioned in other books, it was thought to be beyond rediscovery until a Danish scholar named J. L. Heiberg heard a report about a palimpsest that was located in the monastery of the Holy Sepulchre, in Jerusalem. A palimpsest is a parchment that has been written on more than once, with the original writing still being visible.

Upon examination of the document, Heiberg saw that it contained an Archimedean text. Apparently, a monk living between the twelfth and fourteenth centuries had run out of paper for his prayer book. To remedy this, the monk took pages out of Archimedes' book, washed away the ink, turned the pages sideways, and wrote on them. Of course, in the past, when paper was not as plentiful as it is now, this was a common practice. Luckily, the monk had done a poor job of erasing Archimedes' writing. There was still a faint trace of Archimedes' text, most of which Heiberg was able to decipher. The underlying manuscript contained almost the entire text of the long-lost *The Method*, as well as versions of some of Archimedes' works that had already been rediscovered.

Finding *The Method* has been a key factor to our understanding of what led Archimedes to some of his discoveries. Perhaps there are more of Archimedes' works out there, waiting to be found.

The Archimedes palimpsest is a tenth-century parchment copy of Archimedes' work *The Method*. The parchment of the palimpsest was unbound and used for a Christian prayer book in the twelfth century, and this great mathematical work was almost lost to time. Luckily, most of Archimedes' original text has been recovered in modern times through the use of ultraviolet light and X-rays.

rediscovery goes to a man named Regiomontanus, a Renaissance scientist who was a brilliant mathematician and a gifted linguist. Following the fall of Constantinople in 1453, many Greek-speaking people immigrated to the West, bringing with them ancient manuscripts. Regiomontanus understood the complicated mathematics found in the manuscripts, and he set out to translate them.

Starting in 1471, Regiomontanus began to mass-produce and mass-circulate the key Greek mathematical

Johann Müller, also known as Regiomontanus, translated a number of Archimedes' manuscripts. One of the most important astronomers of the fifteenth century, Regiomontanus also translated many works by other mathematicians. Regiomontanus's translations were consulted by many astronomers, including Galileo and Copernicus.

texts. Though Regiomontanus was killed by the plague that raged through Europe during the fifteenth century, his assistant continued his work. In 1543, Nicolaus Copernicus used those very texts to develop his theory that Earth revolves around the sun. During the mid-sixteenth century, some of Archimedes' more important works were published. The scientific community turned to them with immediate interest.

The works were translated into Italian, as well as Latin, which was the language of the scientists. Archimedes' influence quickly spread through Italy and Europe, and had an impact on some of the greatest minds known to mankind. Galileo Galilei was an Italian astronomer and physicist known for his study of motion. He was interested in things such as falling and rolling objects and projectiles. He took the next step in mechanics, picking up where Archimedes had left off centuries earlier.

A GIANT AMONG MEN

In the centuries following Archimedes' rediscovery, his work has laid the foundation for today's mathematics. Though the details of some of the stories surrounding his life may be more legend than fact, the contribution he made to both theoretical and

This eighteenth-century oil painting by Giuseppe Nogari shows
Archimedes in contemplation. One of the greatest mathematical minds
the world has ever known, Archimedes made great strides in theoretical
mathematics and designed a number of practical inventions. Although
Archimedes' advances were not fully appreciated during his lifetime, his
work changed the way we understand the world.

applied mathematics cannot be denied. Archimedes discovered how to measure a circle, began the idea of developing a system for counting large numbers, and proved the principles of levers. Archimedes also began the sciences of mechanics and hydrostatics, and he discovered the laws of buoyancy and specific gravity. With these, Archimedes set the world on a course that has led to the feats of science we have seen in recent years.

Even before his rediscovery, many scientists were already using Archimedes' works as their foundations. Though only ten of Archimedes' treatises have been recovered, other scientists referenced Archimedes in countless works. Among his lost papers were several addressing the subject of astronomy. This included one entitled *On Sphere-making*, in which Archimedes described the construction of his planetarium.

Although he was considered a great astronomer during his time, Archimedes is not thought of as an astronomer today. However, he was probably a greater contributor to the field of astronomy than we will ever know. Because so many of his works have been lost, we will never know the true extent of Archimedes' influence.

Unlike many ancient mathematicians, Archimedes gained a reputation for his accomplishments in his

own time. However, the true genius of his work is probably appreciated more today than it was then. Today, we have the knowledge of all that was learned by those who came before us. In fact, the greatest scientific ideas of today are based on things that other scientists learned in the past.

Sir Isaac Newton once said, "If I have seen further, it is by standing upon the shoulders of giants." Archimedes had few giants on whose shoulders he could stand. He had only basic ideas and principles. However, Archimedes turned these into true, original scientific works of art. Galileo called him divine, saying that without Archimedes he could have achieved nothing. Archimedes was truly amazing. It is safe to say that when Newton spoke of "giants," he had Archimedes in mind.

TIMELINE

814 BC	Phoenician colonists establish the city of Carthage in North Africa.
733 BC	Greek colonists from Corinth establish the city of Syracuse on the island of Sicily.
332 BC	Alexander the Great establishes the city of Alexandria in northern Egypt.
330 BC	Euclid is born.
323 BC	The Hellenistic period begins with the death of Alexander the Great.
306 BC	Hiero II, future king of Syracuse, is born.
300 BC	Ptolemy builds the Museum of Alexandria.
287 BC	Archimedes is born.
275 BC	Euclid dies.
circa 270 BC	Hiero becomes king of Syracuse.
264 BC	The First Punic War begins.

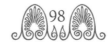

263 BC	King Hiero signs a peace treaty with Rome.
247 BC	Hannibal, the Carthaginian general, is born.
241 BC	The First Punic War ends; Rome gains control of Sicily, except for Syracuse.
230 BC	Hiero's grandson Hieronymus is born.
218 BC	The Second Punic War begins.
215 BC	King Hiero dies; Hieronymus assumes the throne.
215 BC	Hieronymus switches allegiance from Rome to Carthage.
212 BC	Roman leader Marcellus captures Syracuse.
212 BC	Archimedes is killed by a Roman soldier.
75 BC	Cicero discovers and restores Archimedes' tomb.
30 BC	The Hellenistic period ends with Rome's occupation of the last major Hellenistic kingdom.

30 BC	Vitruvius publishes an architecture book containing the story of Archimedes' discovery of the law of buoyancy.
AD 75	Plutarch writes a biography about Marcellus in which is contained a biography of Archimedes.
AD 1471	Regiomontanus begins mass-producing and mass-circulating Greek mathematical texts, including Archimedes' work.
AD 1610	Ludolph van Ceulen calculates pi using a polygon with more than 30 billion sides.
AD 1906	Archimedes' treatise *The Method* is discovered.
AD 1981	Pi is calculated, with a computer, to more than 2 million decimal places.

GLOSSARY

area The measurement of space within given parameters.

circumference The measurement of the outer boundary of a shape.

cone A solid shape that tapers from a round bottom to a sharp point on top.

cylinder A round, elongated solid whose ends are circular.

dimension A measurement in one direction in either space or time.

ellipse A shape that resembles an elongated circle, one whose length is greater than its width.

fortification A fortress or protected area.

geometry A branch of mathematics that calculates shapes and their relationships with one another.

hydraulic Relating to the movement of water or liquid.

muse A poet.

papyrus A tall, aquatic plant whose leaves were often used as writing material.

parabola A shape resembling that of a bowl.

sphere A solid shape that resembles a ball whose distance from the center to the surface is equal at all points.

spiral A curve made by circling a fixed point, either by coming increasingly closer to it or by moving farther away from it.

treatise A written document outlining a particular argument or position.

FOR MORE INFORMATION

Archimedes Home Page
New York University
Courant Institute of Mathematical Sciences
251 Mercer Street
New York, NY 10012
Phone: (212) 998-3513
Web site: http://www.math.nyu.edu/~crorres/
  Archimedes/contents.html

PBS
NOVA/Infinite Secrets
1320 Braddock Place
Alexandria, VA 22314
Web site: http://www.pbs.org/wgbh/nova/archimedes

The Archimedes Project
Stanford University
210 Panama Street
Stanford, CA 94305-4115
(650) 723-1710
Web site: http://archimedes.stanford.edu

WEB SITES

Due to the changing nature of Internet links, the Rosen Publishing Group, Inc., has developed an online list of Web sites related to the subject of this book. This site is updated regularly. Please use this link to access the list:

http://www.rosenlinks.com/lgp/arch

FOR FURTHER READING

Asimov, Isaac. *Great Ideas of Science.* Boston, MA: Houghton Mifflin, 1969.

Bendick, Jeanne. *Archimedes and the Door of Science.* Warsaw, ND: Bethlehem Books, 1995.

Blatner, David. *The Joy of Pi.* New York, NY: Walker, 1997.

Durant, Will. *The Story of Civilization.* New York, NY: Simon & Schuster, 1939.

Hull, Robert E. *Everyday Life: World of Ancient Greece.* Danbury, CT: Grolier Publishing, 1999.

Lafferty, Peter. *Archimedes.* New York, NY: Bookwright, 1991.

McGinnis, Maura. *Greece: A Primary Source Cultural Guide.* New York, NY: Rosen Publishing, 2004.

Pearson, Anne. *Ancient Greece.* New York, NY: Alfred A. Knopf, 1992.

Reimer, Luetta, and Wilbert Reimer. *Mathematicians Are People, Too: Stories from the Live of the Great Mathematicians.* Palo Alto, CA: Dale Seymour Publications, 1990.

Stein, Sherman. *Archimedes: What Did He Do Besides Cry Eureka?* Washington, DC: The Mathematical Association of America, 1999.

Zannos, Susan. *The Life and Times of Archimedes.* Hockessin, DE: Mitchell Lane Publishers, Inc., 2005.

BIBLIOGRAPHY

Cajori, Florian. *A History of Mathematics.* New York, NY: Chelsea Publishing Co., 1991.

Heath, Sir Thomas. *History of Greek Mathematics.* New York, NY: Dover Publications, Inc., 1981.

Ipsen, D. C. *Archimedes: Greatest Scientist of the Ancient World.* Hillside, NJ: Enslow Publishers, Inc., 1988.

Muir, Jane. *Of Men & Numbers: The Story of the Great Mathematicians.* New York, NY: Dover Publications, Inc., 1996.

Toomer, Gerald J. "Archimedes." The New Encyclopedia Britannica, Vol. 13, 1988, pp. 930–931.

INDEX

ABOUT THE AUTHOR

Heather Elizabeth Hasan is a freelance writer from Greencastle, Pennsylvania. She lives there with her husband, Omar, and their son, Samuel. Heather is fascinated by the early great thinkers who established the basis for much of what we know today. She would love to someday travel to places like Syracuse, Italy (Archimedes' birthplace) to see where it all began.

PHOTO CREDITS

Cover, title page Private Collection © Christie's Images/Bridgeman Art Library; cover (inset), title page (inset), pp. 59 (top), 93 ©SSPL/The Image Works; p. 8 (inset) Scala/Art Resource, NY; pp. 8–9 Originally published in Historical Atlas of the World © J. W. Cappelens Forlag A/S, Oslo, Norway, 1962. Maps by Berit Lie. Used with permission of J. W. Cappelens Forlag; p. 10 Musée National, Beirut, Lebanon, Giraudon/Bridgeman Art Library; p. 15 akg-images/Orsi Battaglini; p. 18 Prado, Madrid, Spain/Bridgeman Art Library; p. 20 Bildarchiv Preussischer Kulturbesitz/Art Resource, NY; pp. 21, 36 © The British Library; p. 24 © The American Numismatic Society; pp. 25, 83 The Art Archive/Musée du Louvre Paris/Dagli Orti; p. 26 National Gallery of Ireland; p. 29 Erich Lessing/Art Resource, NY; p. 31 akg-images/Electa; p. 33 © Archivo Iconografico, S.A./Corbis; p. 37 Location Unknown, Ancient Art and Architecture Collection Ltd./Bridgeman Art Library; pp. 42–43, 52–53 Science, Industry & Business Library, The New York Public Library, Astor, Lenox and Tilden Foundations; p. 46 Joannes Meursius, Athenae Batavae (Leiden, 1625). Leiden, Universiteit-sbibliotheek, 662 C 10, p. 343; pp. 54–55 The Vatican Library; p. 59 (bottom) © Horace Bristol/ Corbis; p. 61 Ann Ronan Picture Library/HIP/The Image Works; pp. 62, 80, 89 akg-images; p. 66 © Science Museum/SSPL/The Image Works; pp. 70–71, 92 © Christie's Images Ltd; p. 72 © akg-images/Johann Brandste; pp. 76–77, 81 Galleria degli Uffizi, Florence, Italy/Bridgeman Art Library; pp. 86, 88 © Mary Evans Picture Library/The Image Works; p. 95 Pushkin Museum, Moscow, Russia/Bridgeman Art Library.

Designer: Tahara Anderson

Editor: Nicholas Croce

Photo Researcher: Amy Feinberg